THE BLUEPRINT FOR SUCCESS

"Unlock The Secret to Living Your Best Life, Achieving Wealth"

Introduction,

Welcome, friends! Are you tired of living a mundane, unfulfilling life? Are you ready to take control and manifest the abundance, wealth, health, prosperity, and success that you deserve? I have some exciting news for you - the answer to your prayers is finally here!

This life-changing book is your comprehensive guide to unlocking your full potential and creating the life of your dreams. It's a step-by-step blueprint that will take you on a journey of self-discovery and transformation.

Imagine waking up each day feeling motivated, inspired, and filled with purpose.

Imagine having a boundless supply of energy, wealth, and happiness. Imagine having the power to create and shape your life exactly as you envision it. This is what The Blueprint for Success is all about—giving you the tools and knowledge to tap into the universal forces of abundance and create a truly divine life.

This book is not just a read, it's a journey - a journey that will take you on a deep dive into your inner self and help you discover the true essence of who you are. You will learn how to harness the power of your thoughts, emotions, and beliefs to attract abundance and success into your life. You will discover the secret to unlocking your full potential and living a life filled with purpose, passion, and prosperity.

With its practical tips and powerful chapters of knowledge, this book is guaranteed to transform the way you think, feel, and live. Whether you're just starting on your journey of personal growth or you're already well on your way, this book is the ultimate guide to attracting abundance, wealth, health, prosperity, and success into your life.

So, are you ready to embark on this life-changing journey? Are you ready to create the life of your dreams and tap into the divine forces of abundance? Then let's get started!

Table Of Contents:

Chapter 15: Complementing Exercise with Other Aspects of Life: "Balance your life, align your vibration, live your best life."

Chapter 16: The Power of Health and Strength: "Elevate Your Life: Balance Exercise and Nutrition with Purpose."

Chapter 17: Forgiving and Releasing Negative Emotions: "Release the pain and open the door to a peaceful life."

Chapter 18: Staying in the Moment and Focusing on the Good: "Focus on the Good and Reap the Rewards."

Chapter 19: Finding and Expressing Your Life Purpose: "Live life with purpose and intention - Unlock your potential"

Chapter 20: The Law of Polarity and the Present Moment: "Let go of the past, embrace the present: live an epic life."

Chapter 21: Happiness as a Process: "Discover your happiness: A journey to self-discovery."

Chapter 22: Pursuing Dreams and Overcoming Fears: "Turn failures into opportunities, chase your dreams with passion."

Chapter 23: Creating or Disintegrating: "Create the future, shape your legacy."

Chapter 24: Embracing Abundance and Joy: "Celebrate your wins and live life to the fullest."

Chapter 25: Appreciating the Journey: "Discover beauty in every step of the way!"

Chapter 26: The Power of Positive Thinking: "Harness the power of positive thinking - create an epic life filled with joy, abundance, and fulfillment"

Chapter 27: The Importance of Self-Care: "Find Balance, Find Bliss: Embrace the Art of Self-Care."

Chapter 28: Building Strong Relationships: "From strangers to lifelong friends - Connect with the heart, listen with the soul"

Chapter 29: Learning from Life's Challenges: "Embrace the unknown, cultivate resilience, and unleash your full potential."

Chapter 30: Living with Purpose and Passion: "Believe in yourself, the sky's the limit."

In Conclusion

Chapter 1:

Introduction to the Mehta Secret:

"Unlock Your Inner Wealth, Unleash Your Abundant Life"

Here's why you should start using the Mehta Secret right now:

The Mehta Secret is a captivating concept that has been shrouded in mystery for centuries. It is an ancient understanding of the universe, and it holds the key to unlocking the door to true wealth, abundance, and happiness.

The word "Mehta" is an enigmatic term referring to a set of metaphysical rules and understandings that cannot be perceived with the physical eye. It's a word that has been passed down through generations and guarded as one of the most precious secrets in human history.

The Mehta Secret is about understanding the difference between the outside world and inner wealth. Most people in this world are programmed to let the outside world control their lives, but the Mehta secret teaches us that true wealth and abundance come from within. We've been taught that we have to work hard, accumulate money and material possessions, and strive for success to be happy. However, the Mehta secret reveals that this is just an illusion and that true wealth and happiness come from within.

To unlock the Mehta secret, we must First, understand the concept of inner wealth. This means that we must delve into our minds and uncover the true essence of who we are. We must learn to recognize our strengths and weaknesses and understand how they play a role in our lives. We must also develop a deep connection with our inner selves and learn to trust our intuition and inner guidance.

Once we have established a connection with our inner selves, we can then begin to tap into the infinite source of abundance and wealth that exists within us. We will learn to understand that money and material possessions are just external representations of the wealth that we already have within us.

We will discover that the key to unlocking our Inner wealth is to cultivate a positive and abundant mindset and to develop an attitude of gratitude and appreciation for all the blessings that we already have in our lives.

The Mehta Secret is a powerful and transformative understanding of the universe that can change your life in ways you never thought possible. By unlocking the secrets of the Mehta, you can tap into an infinite source of inner wealth, abundance, and happiness, and live a life of prosperity, joy, and fulfillment.

If you're ready to transform your life and tap into the infinite source of wealth and abundance within you, then it's time to start using the information about the Mehta Secret. Embrace your journey of self-discovery and unleash the wealth and abundance within you!

Why you should be using the Mehta,

1. Unlock Your Inner Potential: By following the tips and principles of the Mehta Secret, you'll be able to tap into your full potential and unleash the wealth and abundance within you. Discover your strengths and weaknesses, connect with your inner self, and cultivate a positive and abundant mindset.

2. Attract More Abundance and Wealth: The Mehta Secret teaches us that true wealth and abundance come from within. By embracing a positive and abundant mindset, practicing gratitude and appreciation, and letting go of the outside world, you'll attract more abundance and wealth into your life.

3. Live a Life of Fulfillment and Joy: The Mehta Secret is all about living a life of prosperity, joy, and fulfillment. By tapping into the infinite source of wealth and abundance within you, you'll be able to live a life that is rich with joy, love, and happiness.

4. Break Free from Limitations: Most people let the outside world control their lives, but the Mehta Secret teaches us to break free from these limitations and tap into the infinite source of inner wealth and abundance. By following the tips and principles of the Mehta Secret, you'll be able to break free from the limitations that have been holding you back and live a life of freedom and abundance.

5. Cultivate a Positive Mindset: The first step towards unlocking the Mehta secret is to cultivate a positive and abundant mindset. Focus on the things that you're grateful for and surround yourself with positive people and experiences. A positive mindset will help you attract more abundance and wealth into your life.

6. Connect with Your Inner Self: To tap into the wealth and abundance within you, you must first establish a connection with your inner self. Take time to meditate, journal, or do other activities that allow you to reflect on your thoughts and feelings. Get to know yourself on a deeper level and trust your intuition and inner guidance.

7. Practice Gratitude and Appreciation: One of the key principles of the Mehta secret is to develop an attitude of gratitude and appreciation. Make it a habit to express gratitude for the blessings in your life, no matter how big or small. This will help you attract more abundance and wealth into your life. Embrace Your Strengths and Weaknesses: It's important to embrace both your strengths and weaknesses to unlock the Mehta secret. Acknowledge your strengths and work on improving your weaknesses. By embracing all aspects of yourself, you'll be able to tap into your full potential and unlock your inner wealth.

8. Let Go of the Outside World: Most people let the outside world control their lives, but the Mehta secret teaches us that true wealth and abundance come from within. Let go of the things that are holding you back and focus on cultivating a positive and abundant mindset.

By following these tips, you'll be well on your way to unlocking the secrets of the Mehta and tapping into the infinite source of inner wealth, abundance, and happiness. So go ahead and embrace your journey of self-discovery and unlock the wealth and abundance within you today!

Chapter 2: Defining Wealth
"Define, Plan, Learn, Succeed"

When it comes to defining wealth, everyone has a unique perspective. For some, it might be the ability to live without worrying about money. For others, it could be the freedom to travel the world or the luxury of owning a yacht.

For me, wealth is a combination of both financial stability and personal satisfaction. It's not just about having a high net worth or owning multiple properties, but it's about having the peace of mind and comfort to live the life I desire, without financial worries.

Now, the key to unlocking the "Mehta secret" of wealth lies in first determining what wealth means to you. Once you have a clear definition, you can set a goal and take the necessary steps to achieve it.

For some, financial independence might mean having enough savings to cover all their expenses, without having to worry about relying on a steady income. Others might see financial independence as being able to retire early or being able to work on their terms, without having to answer a boss.

For those who aspire to own a yacht, it could be a symbol of luxury, prestige, and adventure. It could be a goal that they strive to achieve, not just because of the material possessions, but because of the experiences and memories it would bring to their lives. Ultimately, the path to wealth is different for everyone, but the first step remains the same: defining what it means to you.

Once you have a clear definition, you can start taking concrete steps towards achieving it, whether that means saving more, investing in stocks and cryptocurrency, or starting your own business. With focus, determination, and a plan in place, you too can unlock the secret of wealth and live the life of your dreams.

Here are some tips that are tried and true.

1. Get crystal clear on what wealth means to you: Before you can start building wealth, you need to have a clear understanding of what it means to you. Take the time to think deeply about what you value most, and what you want your life to look like. Do you want financial security? Freedom to travel? The ability to give back to your community? Once you know what wealth means to you, you can create a roadmap for getting there.

2. Set realistic and attainable goals: Wealth-building is a marathon, not a sprint, so it's important to set realistic and attainable goals. This will help you stay motivated and focused, and it will give you a roadmap to follow. Whether you're aiming to save a certain amount of money, pay off debt, or invest in stocks, be sure to set achievable goals that you can work towards.

3. Make a plan and stick to it: A goal without a plan is just a wish, so it's important to create a solid plan for building wealth. This might mean creating a budget, automating your savings, or seeking out financial advice from a professional. Whatever it is, make a plan and stick to it.

4. Learn, learn, learn: Building wealth is not a one-time event, it's a lifelong journey. And just like any journey, it requires education and continuous learning. Whether you're reading books, taking courses, or attending seminars, be sure to educate yourself and stay up to date on the latest financial strategies and trends.

5. Stay disciplined and focused: Building wealth takes discipline and focus, so it's important to stay focused on your goals. This means avoiding unnecessary expenses, sticking to your budget, and making smart financial decisions. Remember, every penny you save today is one penny closer to your financial goals.

With these tips in mind, you're well on your way to unlocking the secrets of wealth. Whether you're just starting or you're a seasoned pro, these tips will help you define your path to financial freedom and live the life you've always dreamed of. So, get started today, and see just how far you can go!

Chapter 3: Mindset for Wealth

"Believe in yourself, Gratitude, Clarity, Law of correspondence, trusting your attraction, and Taking Action"

The key to unlocking wealth and abundance in one's life lies in their mindset. When it comes to acquiring wealth, it's not just about what you do, but also how you think about it. And that's where the importance of a wealthy mindset comes in. It's about shifting your thoughts and beliefs to align with abundance so that you can attract more prosperity into your life.

One of the most important aspects of a wealthy mindset is belief in yourself. You have to truly believe that you deserve to be rich and that you have the capability to create wealth in your life. It's about recognizing your self-worth and having faith in your abilities. When you believe in yourself, you become unstoppable.

Gratitude is another essential component of a wealth mindset. Being grateful for what you have, no matter how small it may seem, sets the stage for more abundance to flow into your life. When you cultivate an attitude of gratitude, you radiate positivity and attract more positivity into your life.

Clarity is also crucial when it comes to creating a wealth mindset. You must have a clear abundance and that you deserve it, that's what you'll attract. It's all about shifting your as you align your thoughts and beliefs with it. Trusting in your attraction means letting go of the need to control every aspect of your life and having faith that things will work out in your favor. Faith that the universe will bring you the wealth and abundance that you desire, as long as your thoughts and beliefs align with abundance.

Another key aspect of a wealthy mindset is trust in your attraction. This means having a vision of what you want to achieve and being laser-focused on your goals. When you have clarity, you have a roadmap that guides you toward success, and you're able to take action with purpose and intention.

The Law of Correspondence is also an important aspect of a wealth mindset. This law states that your thoughts and beliefs create your reality. So, if you believe that wealth is scarce, that's exactly what you'll attract into your life.

Finally, taking action is an essential component of a wealthy mindset. No matter how positive your thoughts and beliefs may be, they won't create wealth in your life unless you take action to make it happen. It's about taking inspired action, not just any action, but action that is aligned with your goals and vision.

A wealth mindset is about aligning your thoughts and beliefs with abundance, having faith in yourself and your abilities, being grateful for what you have, having clarity about what you want, trusting in your attraction, and taking inspired action. By embracing these principles, you'll be able to attract wealth and abundance into your life and create the life of your dreams.

Here are some tips and takeaways from this chapter to help you align your thoughts and beliefs with abundance.

1. Let's start with belief in yourself. To cultivate this, it's important to practice self-affirmation and positive self-talk. Every morning, stand in front of the mirror, look yourself in the eye, and say out loud, "I am worthy of wealth and abundance." Repeat this several times, until you truly believe it. This simple exercise will help you to build your self-confidence and increase your belief in yourself.

2. Have gratitude. To cultivate this, start a gratitude journal. Every day, write down three things that you're grateful for. It could be something as simple as a good cup of coffee, or as complex as a new job opportunity. This exercise will help you to focus on the positive and attract more positivity into your life.

3. When it comes to clarity, visualization is your best friend. Close your eyes and imagine yourself living the life of your dreams. What does it look like? What does it feel like? The more vivid the visualization, the better. This exercise will help you to focus on your goals and give you the clarity you need to make them a reality.

4. The Law of Correspondence is all about shifting your thoughts and beliefs to align with abundance. To cultivate this, make a conscious effort to focus on positive thoughts and beliefs. If a negative thought pops into your head, replace it with a positive one. This takes practice, but over time, you'll find that you're able to shift your thoughts and beliefs and attract more wealth and abundance into your life.

5. When it comes to trusting your attraction, the key is to let go of control. Instead of trying to control every aspect of your life, let go, and trust that the universe will bring you what you desire. This takes faith, but over time, you'll find that things start to work out in your favor and that wealth and abundance come to you more easily.

6. Taking action is crucial. To make your dreams a reality, you have to take inspired action. This means taking steps that are aligned with your goals and taking action with purpose and intention. Start small and take one step at a time. Over time, you'll find that your wealth and abundance grow and that you're able to create the life of your dreams.

In conclusion, these are just a few tips to help you cultivate a wealth mindset.

Remember, it's all about shifting your thoughts and beliefs to align with abundance, having faith in yourself and your abilities, being grateful for what you have, having clarity about what you want, trusting in your attraction, and taking inspired action. With these principles in mind, you'll be well on your way to creating the life of your dreams and attracting wealth and abundance into your life.

Chapter 4:
"Tools and Methodologies"

"Transform Your Financial Future with The Mehta Secret"

The Mehta secret is a unique approach to unlocking our potential and discovering the wealth that is truly available to us. It's more than just a set of tools or methodologies - it's a way of understanding the world and the abundance that surrounds us.

At the core of the Mehta secret is the belief that wealth is a birthright. This means that every one of us is entitled to live a life filled with abundance and prosperity.

Unfortunately, many of us have been taught to believe that wealth is something that only a select few can attain. This limiting belief can hold us back from truly experiencing the wealth and abundance that is available to us.

But, when we embrace the idea that wealth is a birthright, we can start to break free from these limiting beliefs. We can begin to see the world through a new lens and understand that abundance is truly available to us.

The Mehta secret combines a variety of tools and methodologies to help us unlock our wealth potential. These may include techniques for visualization and manifestation, financial planning strategies, and ways to cultivate a wealth-focused mindset. The key is to use these tools and methodologies in a holistic and integrated way so that they work together to help us achieve our financial goals.

One of the most powerful aspects of the Mehta secret is its focus on personal growth and self-discovery.

By looking inward and exploring our thoughts and beliefs, we can gain a deeper understanding of the limiting beliefs that may be holding us back from experiencing true wealth and abundance.

The Mehta secret is a unique and transformative approach to wealth creation. By combining tools and methodologies with a wealth-focused mindset, we can unlock our birthright to abundance and live the life we truly desire. So, if you're ready to start experiencing the wealth and abundance that is truly available to you, it's time to start exploring the Mehta secret!

Here are some tips to help you get started on your journey.

1. Embrace the idea of wealth as a birthright. Remember, you are entitled to live a life filled with abundance and prosperity. When you believe this to be true, you'll start to see the world differently and be more open to the abundance that surrounds you.

2. Get to know yourself. The Mehta secret places a strong emphasis on personal growth and self-discovery. Take some time to reflect on your thoughts and beliefs about money and wealth and see if any limiting beliefs are holding you back from experiencing abundance.

3. Take action. The Mehta secret is about more than just dreaming of wealth - it's about taking action to make it a reality. Whether it's creating a budget, investing in yourself, or seeking out new financial opportunities, take steps towards your wealth goals every day.

4. Cultivate a wealth-focused mindset. Believe in your ability to create wealth, and surround yourself with positive, abundance-focused people who support your goals.

5. Use the tools and methodologies of the Mehta secret holistically. Visualization, manifestation, and financial planning strategies are just a few of the tools you can use to unlock your wealth potential. The key is to use them in a way that works for you and fits your unique needs and goals.

6. Celebrate your successes. No matter how big or small they may be, celebrate every step you take towards experiencing abundance and prosperity. This will help keep you motivated and focused on your wealth goals.

secret. Remember, wealth and abundance are truly available to you - all you have to do is believe it, take action, and embrace the power of the Mehta secret!

So, there you have it! A few tips to help you get started on your journey with the Mehta.

Chapter 5:
Aligning Thoughts and Beliefs

"The journey to abundance starts with a clear vision"

Creating a life of abundance and wealth is a journey that requires a combination of aligning your thoughts and beliefs, building something of true excellence, and having a selling proposition that creates value for others.

To understand the secrets to unlocking this life, we must delve into the principles that guide it.

First, it is essential to align your thoughts and beliefs with what you want your life to be. This means having a clear vision of what you want to achieve and then aligning your thoughts and actions with that vision. Your thoughts and beliefs are like the compass that guides you toward your goals, so it's crucial to make sure that they are aligned with what you want to achieve.

Second, to create a life of abundance, you must build something of true excellence. This means dedicating yourself to your craft and investing the time, energy, and effort necessary to create something that stands out. Whether it's a business, a product, or a service, the key is to focus on excellence and create something that people will value and appreciate.

Third, it's essential to have a selling proposition that is both aggressive and creates value for others. Marketing and promoting your work is essential if you want to attract wealth and abundance. However, it's not just about selling; it's about creating value for others and providing a service that meets their needs.

Finally, it's crucial to understand that the law of attraction doesn't happen on its own. Attracting wealth and abundance requires action, clarity, and trust. You must take action towards your goals, have a clear vision of what you want to achieve, and trust in the process.

Aligning your thoughts and beliefs, building something of true excellence, having a selling proposition that creates value for others, and understanding the law of attraction are the key principles to unlocking the secrets to a life of wealth and abundance. The journey may be challenging, but with dedication and a commitment to these principles, you can achieve the life you desire.

Are you ready to unlock the secrets to a life of abundance and prosperity?

Then, let's get started with these tips and this chapter that will help you align your thoughts and beliefs, build something of true excellence, and create a selling proposition that delivers value to others.

1. Get crystal clear on your vision: The first step to aligning your thoughts and beliefs is to get crystal clear on what you want to achieve. Write down your goals and dreams and visualize them as if they have already happened. This will help you focus your thoughts and beliefs on what you want to create in your life.

2. Invest in your craft: To build something of true excellence, you must invest time, energy, and effort into your craft. Whether it's a business, product, or service, take the time to perfect your skills, and continually strive to improve and innovate.

3. Create a unique selling proposition: What sets you apart from the competition? What makes your product or service unique and valuable? This is your unique selling proposition (USP), and it's essential to have one if you want to stand out in the marketplace.

4. Put yourself out there: To create value for others, you must put yourself out there and market your work aggressively. Don't be afraid to network, promote your work, and reach out to potential customers.
The more you put yourself out there, the more opportunities you'll have to create value and service for others.

5. Take inspired action: Understanding the law of attraction is one thing but putting it into practice is another. To attract wealth and abundance, you must take inspired action towards your goals. This means taking steps each day to bring your vision to life and trusting in the process.

6. Celebrate your wins: Don't forget to celebrate your wins along the way! Achieving your goals and creating a life of abundance is a journey, and it's important to acknowledge and celebrate your progress.

In conclusion, aligning your thoughts and beliefs, building something of true excellence, and creating a selling proposition that delivers value to others are the key principles to unlocking the secrets to a life of wealth and abundance. So, get ready to take inspired action, celebrate your wins, and start living the life you've always dreamed of!

Chapter 6:

The Mehta Secret in Relationships

"Love is the ultimate connection: Embrace the Mehta secret to relationships."

Love is a magical and powerful force that can bring people together and help them create strong and meaningful relationships. Relationships can be one of the most rewarding experiences in life, but they can also be one of the most challenging.

That's why it's important to understand the essence of relationships, and the Mehta secret to relationships is to understand that the universe is always giving you love in exchange for the love that you give.

When we give love, we are not just talking about showering our partners with gifts or compliments, but about a deep and abiding sense of connection, appreciation, and respect. Love is a two-way street, and it requires effort from both parties to make it work. When both partners are willing to give and receive love, their relationship becomes stronger, more resilient, and more fulfilling.

However, love can also be a vulnerable and fragile thing. People are often afraid of giving love because they fear that they will not receive it in return. They worry that they will be hurt or rejected, and this can make it difficult for them to open up to their partners and show their love.

That's why it's so important to understand the Mehta secret to relationships. Love is not just about receiving what you want, but also about giving. When you are willing to give love, even if you are not sure that you will receive it in return, you are opening yourself up to the universe and inviting it to bring love into your life.

The Mehta's secret to relationships is to understand that love is the essence of relationships. Love is a two-way street that requires effort from both partners, and it can be a powerful and transformative force in our lives. When we are willing to give love, even when we are unsure of the outcome, we are opening ourselves up to a world of possibilities and inviting the universe to bring us the love that we deserve.

Here are some tips to help to use The Mehta Secret in your relationships.

1. Practice Gratitude: The first step in giving love is to practice gratitude. When you are thankful for what you have and for the love in your life, it becomes easier to give love to others. Start each day by writing down three things that you are grateful for, and make sure to express your gratitude to your partner on a regular basis.

2. Embrace vulnerability: Love is a vulnerable thing, and it requires you to open up and be honest with your partner. Don't be afraid to express your feelings, even if they are not easy to share. Your partner will appreciate your honesty and will be more likely to return the love that you give.

3. Listen actively: One of the best ways to give love is to listen to your partner. Show them that you care by truly listening to what they have to say and asking questions to show that you are engaged and interested in what they are saying.

4. Be present: In today's fast-paced world, it's easy to get caught up in our phones and other distractions, but it's important to be present with your partner. Put away your phone and focus on your partner, giving them your full attention and presence.

5. Practice kindness: Kindness is a simple yet powerful way to give love. Do something small each day to show your partner that you care, like bringing them a cup of coffee in the morning or leaving a love note in their lunchbox.

6. Make time for each other: Life can get busy, but it's important to make time for your partner. Plan a date night, take a walk together, or simply sit down and have a conversation without any distractions.

7. Celebrate your love: Finally, celebrate your love! Acknowledge the love that you have for each other and celebrate it in small and big ways. Write love letters, take romantic vacations, or simply tell each other why you love each other.

By following these tips, you can master the Mehta secret to relationships and experience the full power of love in your life. Remember, love is a two-way street, so be open and willing to give love, and the universe will bring love into your life in return.

Chapter 7
The Importance of Self-Love

"Be your own best friend, love yourself wholeheartedly"

Self-love is a crucial aspect of one's personal growth and well-being. It's the act of treating oneself with kindness, compassion, and respect, just as you would your closest friend. It's about recognizing your worth and value and believing in yourself.

Self-love begins with self-awareness, and taking the time to understand your thoughts, feelings, and emotions. It's important to acknowledge both the positive and negative aspects of yourself and to make peace with who you are, flaws and all. By embracing your authentic self, you can build a strong foundation for self-love.

Negative self-talk can be incredibly damaging, holding you back from reaching your full potential. It's important to challenge these thoughts and replace them with positive, empowering ones. Surround yourself with people who support and uplift you and try to focus on the things you are proud of, rather than your weaknesses.

It's also important to take care of yourself, both physically and emotionally. This can include exercising regularly, eating a healthy diet, getting enough sleep, and engaging in activities that bring you joy and fulfillment. By doing so, you'll have the energy and positive mindset to tackle any challenges that come your way.

Finally, self-love is not a one-time event, but a continuous process that requires effort and dedication. It's about loving yourself, even on your worst days, and being patient and forgiving with yourself.

It's about realizing that you are deserving of love and happiness and making it a priority in your life.

Self-love is the foundation of a strong relationship, not just with others, but with yourself. By treating yourself with love and respect, you'll build a strong, resilient, and confident self that is capable of overcoming any obstacle that comes your way. So, go ahead, be kind to yourself, believe in yourself, and watch your life transform in ways you never thought possible.

Self-love is a journey, and like all journeys, it requires effort and dedication. However, the rewards are immeasurable, and the benefits can be life changing.

Here are some tips and takeaways to help you get started on your self-love journey:

1. Practice self-awareness: Take the time to understand your thoughts, and feelings, and uplift yourself. Focus on the things you are proud of and make an effort to ignore the negativity.

2. Take care of yourself: Exercise regularly, eat a healthy diet, get enough sleep, and engage in activities that bring you joy and fulfillment. By doing so, you'll have the energy and positive mindset to tackle any challenges that come your way.

3. Be patient and forgiving Self-love is a continuous process that requires effort and dedication. Be patient with yourself and forgive yourself for your mistakes.

4. Practice gratitude: Focus on the things in your life that you are grateful for and try to appreciate them every day.

5. Celebrate your successes: No matter how small they may be, take the time to celebrate your successes. Recognize your achievements and be proud of yourself.

6. Treat yourself with kindness: Treat yourself with the same kindness, compassion, and respect that you would show to your closest friend.

7. Challenge negative self-talk: Negative self-talk can hold you back from reaching your full potential. Challenge these thoughts and replace them with positive, empowering ones.

By following these tips, you'll be well on your way to building a strong, resilient, and confident self. Remember, self-love is a journey, and it's not a destination that you'll reach overnight. Be kind to yourself, believe in yourself, and watch your life transform in ways you never thought possible.

Chapter 8: Relationships as a Gift

"Life's most beautiful journey awaits – embrace relationships with open arms."

Relationships are one of the most beautiful and complex aspects of life and approaching them with gratitude and positivity can make all the difference. The idea that you need someone else to make your life worthwhile is simply not true, and it's important to believe in yourself and your worth. That being said, the gift of a relationship should not be taken lightly, as it has the power to bring immense joy, growth, and fulfillment to our lives.

It's easy to get caught up in the idea that finding someone to share our lives with will magically fix all of our problems and make everything right, but that simply isn't the case. Relationships are not a magic cure-all, but they can provide an incredible source of support and companionship as we navigate through life's ups and downs. They give us the opportunity to share our experiences, our laughter, and our tears with someone who truly understands us.

One of the most important things to keep in mind when it comes to relationships is that they are not a destination, but rather a journey. The journey of a relationship is one filled with twists, turns, and unexpected detours, but it's these detours that often lead to the most beautiful experiences. Whether it's discovering new interests or passions, or simply learning to be a better person, the journey of a relationship can bring about incredible growth and personal development.

It's also important to remember that relationships require effort, patience, and most importantly, communication. Relationships are not always easy, and it's natural to encounter obstacles and challenges along the way, but it's how we choose to handle these challenges that can make all the difference.

Open and honest communication is key, and it's essential to approach each obstacle with a positive attitude, a willingness to listen and understand, and a deep commitment to the relationship.

Relationships are a gift from the universe and should be approached with gratitude, positivity, and a deep understanding of what they truly are – a journey filled with beautiful experiences, growth, and personal development. Remember that life is full of ups and downs and that it's not always necessary to have someone else to make your life worthwhile. Believe in yourself, trust in the journey, and enjoy the ride.

Relationships are a beautiful and complex part of life and approaching them with the right mindset can make all the difference.

Here are some tips and takeaways to help you.

1. Believe in yourself: Before you can have a successful relationship, you must first believe in your own worth and value. Don't rely on someone else to make your life worthwhile – have faith in yourself and your own journey.

2. Embrace the journey: Relationships are not a destination, but a journey filled with twists and turns. Embrace the ups and downs and see each experience as an opportunity for growth and personal development.

3. Communicate openly: Communication is key in any relationship. Make sure to approach each obstacle with an open mind and a willingness to listen and understand.

4. Practice patience: Relationships take time, effort, and patience. Don't expect things to happen overnight and be patient with yourself and your partner as you navigate through the journey together.

5. Find joy in the little things: Relationships are filled with countless little moments that bring joy and happiness. Take the time to appreciate these moments and savor the memories.

6. Be grateful: Relationships are a gift, and it's important to approach them with gratitude and appreciation for what they bring to our lives.

7. Have fun: Relationships should be fun, and filled with laughter, adventure, and joy. Don't take things too seriously, and always make time for fun and play.

8. Be supportive: Relationships are about support and companionship. Be there for your partner through thick and thin and be willing to lend a hand when needed.

By following these tips, you'll be able to approach relationships with gratitude, positivity, personal development, and joy. So go ahead, take the leap, and enjoy the ride

Chapter 9:
Creating a Stronger Relationship

"Elevate your relationship to new heights."

When it comes to creating a stronger
relationship, it's all about putting in the effort
to understand the other person and make a
genuine connection. By being fully present in
the moment and paying close attention to the
other person's cues, you can form a deeper bond
that will lead to a more fulfilling relationship.

One of the most important things you can do is to be genuinely interested in the other person. Take the time to learn about their interests, their goals, their fears, and their dreams. Ask them questions and listen to their answers with an open heart and mind. When you show that you care about someone and are invested in their well-being, they will feel valued and appreciated.

To stay in the present moment and respond to the other person's feedback and mannerisms, it's essential to remain mindful and focused. Put away your distractions and focus solely on the conversation. Observe the other person's body language and tone of voice and use these cues to tailor your response. When you're fully present, you'll be able to respond more effectively and create a deeper connection.

Another key aspect of creating a stronger relationship is to express the qualities you desire. When you lead by example and show that you value kindness, honesty, and open communication, you'll attract those same qualities in your partner. It's important to remember that relationships are a two-way street, and you can't expect to receive what you're not willing to give.

By paying attention to and being interested in the other person, staying in the present moment, and expressing the qualities you desire in a relationship, you'll be able to create a stronger and deeper connection that will lead to a more fulfilling relationship. Whether you're just starting a new relationship or looking to reignite the spark in a long-term partnership, these simple steps can make a big difference.
Creating a stronger relationship can be a challenge, but it's also one of the most Rewarding things you can do for yourself and your partner.

Here are some tips to help you build a deeper connection and foster a more fulfilling relationship:

1. Put your phone away: When you're having a conversation with your partner, make sure you're fully present and focused on them. Putting away your phone and other distractions will show your partner that you value and respect their time and attention.

2. Ask open-ended questions: Ask your partner about their interests, goals, and dreams. Show that you're genuinely interested in what they have to say and be an active listener.

3. Share your thoughts and feelings: Be open and honest with your partner about what you're feeling and thinking. When you share your thoughts and feelings, you create a deeper sense of intimacy and trust.

4. Be mindful of your body language: Pay attention to your own body language and the way you're holding yourself. When you adopt an open and relaxed posture, you'll communicate a sense of comfort and confidence.

5. Practice active listening: When your partner is talking, listen to what they're saying and respond in a way that shows you understand and empathize with their perspective.

6. Show appreciation: Make sure you let your partner know how much you appreciate them. Whether it's through small gestures, kind words, or physical affection, showing appreciation will strengthen your bond.

7. Lead by example: If you want to cultivate a relationship filled with kindness, honesty, and open communication, make sure you're leading by example. When you embody these qualities, you'll attract them to your partner.

By following these tips and being intentional about building a deeper connection with your partner, you'll be able to create a stronger and more fulfilling relationship. So go ahead, put these tips into practice, and watch as your relationship grows stronger and more vibrant every day!

Chapter 10: Overcoming Criticism

"Embrace criticism, evolve, and soar to new heights."

Dealing with criticism from others can be a tricky and challenging task, but it is a crucial part of life that can help us grow and improve. Criticism is not always a bad thing and can be used as a tool to help us better ourselves, but it is important to know how to handle it properly, so it doesn't damage our self-esteem or relationships.

First and foremost, it's important to understand that criticism often stems from the critic's own insecurities and their own feelings of inadequacy. They may be projecting their own feelings onto you and using criticism as a way to make themselves feel better. It is important not to internalize the criticism and instead try to understand where it is coming from.

When someone gives you feedback, it's important to thank them for taking the time to share their thoughts with you. This will show that you appreciate their input and will also help to defuse any negative emotions that might be present. Whether you choose to accept or reject the criticism, it's important to do so respectfully and without letting it impact your relationship with the person.

One way to handle criticism is to take a step back and examine it objectively. Consider whether there is any truth to the feedback and whether it will help you grow or improve in some way. If you do decide to accept the criticism, be sure to use it constructively to make positive changes in your life. On the other hand, if you reject the criticism, don't let it bring you down.
Instead, focus on your own strengths and what makes you unique and valuable.

Another way to overcome criticism is to surround yourself with positive and supportive people. Seek out friends, family members, or mentors who will uplift you and help you stay motivated. They will provide you with the encouragement and support you need to overcome criticism and maintain your self-esteem.

Criticism from others can be difficult to handle, but it's important to remember that it's often a reflection of the critic's own insecurities and not a true reflection of your worth.

Thank the person for their feedback, accept or reject it objectively, and don't let it impact your relationship. Instead, focus on your own strengths. Embrace the feedback and try to see criticism as a tool for growth and improvement.

If you're looking to overcome criticism and handle it with grace and confidence,

Here are some tips and takeaways to help you navigate the sometimes-rough waters of criticism and emerge as a better, more resilient version of yourself.

positive and supportive people who will help you overcome criticism and maintain your

1. Maintain a healthy balance: Take care of your physical and mental health by engaging in regular exercise, eating a balanced diet, and getting enough sleep. This can help you maintain your energy levels and resilience, even in the face of criticism.

2. Find your inner peace: Cultivate inner peace and calm by engaging in activities that bring you joy and happiness. This can help you maintain your equanimity in the face of criticism and reduce its impact on your well-being.

3. Thank the person for their feedback rather than take it as a personal attack. Ask for clarification if you don't understand the feedback and use it to make positive changes in your life.

4. Keep perspective: Remember that criticism is often a reflection of the critic's own a thick skin can help you handle criticism with grace and reduce the impact it has on your self-esteem.

5. Seek out positive relationships: Surround yourself with positive, supportive people who uplift you and help you stay motivated. These relationships can provide a source of strength and encouragement during difficult times.

6. Practice gratitude: Start each day by listing three things you're grateful for.

   This simple act can help you maintain a positive outlook and perspective, even in the face of criticism.

7. Develop a thick skin: Criticism is inevitable, but it doesn't have to hurt. Developing

By following these tips, you can handle criticism with confidence and come out stronger on the other side. Remember, criticism is a part of life, but it doesn't have to define you. So, take a deep breath, embrace the feedback, and keep on striving towards your goals and aspirations!

Chapter 11:
Balancing Masculine and Feminine Energy

Balancing masculine and feminine energy is a
key aspect of personal growth and
development. This is because everything in
the universe, including human beings,
consists of both masculine and feminine
elements. When these elements are balanced,
they create a harmonious and fulfilling life,
both individually and in relationships.

Masculine energy is often associated with qualities such as assertiveness, independence, and logical thinking. On the other hand, feminine energy is often associated with qualities such as intuition, emotional intelligence, and empathy. Both of these energies are important and necessary, and it is essential to find a balance between them.

Finding a balance between masculine and feminine energies requires a deep understanding of who you are and what makes you unique. This is because each individual embodies different levels of both energies. By embracing all aspects of your personality, you can create a harmonious balance between your masculine and feminine energies.

In relationships, balancing masculine and feminine energies is equally important. When both partners have a balanced energy, they complement each other and create a harmonious dynamic. However, when one partner dominates the relationship with their energy, it can lead to conflict and disharmony.

It is important to recognize that masculine and feminine energies are not limited to gender. Anyone can embody both energies, regardless of their gender identity.

By understanding and embracing your unique balance of masculine and feminine energies, you can create a fulfilling and harmonious life, both within yourself and in your relationships.

Balancing masculine and feminine energies is a crucial aspect of personal growth and development. By embracing all aspects of your personality and finding balance within yourself, you can create a harmonious life filled with joy and fulfillment.

In relationships, a balanced energy dynamic leads to a harmonious dynamic, creating a fulfilling partnership. So, embrace your unique balance of masculine and feminine energies and allow them to complement each other in all aspects of your life.

Here are a few tips for finding balance in your own life and relationships:

1. Self-Reflection: Start by taking a deep dive into your personality and identifying which aspects of your personality embody masculine and feminine energies. Reflect on how these energies play out in your daily life and how they impact your relationships.

2. Embrace Your Uniqueness: Once you have a clear understanding of your own balance of masculine and feminine energies, embrace all aspects of your personality. Allow yourself to be fully expressed and do not be afraid to showcase both your masculine and feminine sides.

3. Practice Self-Care: Taking care of yourself is crucial in finding balance. Engage in activities that nourish your soul and bring you peace, such as meditation, yoga, or journaling. By taking care of yourself, you can cultivate a strong connection to your feminine energy and ensure that you are in a balanced state.

4. Communicate with Your Partner: Communication is key in any relationship, and it is no different when it comes to balancing masculine and feminine energies. Have open and honest conversations with your partner about your balance of energies and how you can work together to create a harmonious dynamic.

5. Embrace Diversity: Remember that masculine and feminine energies are not limited to gender. Embrace the diverse balance of energies within yourself and others. Celebrate the unique ways in which each individual embodies both energies and do not be afraid to learn from those around you.

6. Seek Support: Balancing masculine and feminine energies can be a challenging process, and seeking support from a trusted friend or therapist can be incredibly helpful. Having someone to talk to and work through challenges with can make all the difference in finding balance in your life.

In conclusion, balancing masculine and feminine energies is an ongoing process that requires self-reflection, self-care, open communication, and a willingness to embrace diversity and seek support. By following these tips, you can find a harmonious balance within yourself and in your relationships, creating a fulfilling and joyful life.

Chapter 12:
Introduction to the Law of Gender and Forgiveness

"Be the Change You Wish to See: The Importance of Self-Awareness and Forgiveness."

The Law of Gender and Forgiveness are two powerful concepts that have a profound impact on our relationships and the quality of our lives. Understanding the law of gender is crucial to building strong and fulfilling relationships, whether it be with a romantic partner, a family member, or a friend.

The law of gender states that every person, thing, and event in our lives has a unique energy or vibration that can be masculine or feminine.

Appreciating this law helps us to understand why certain relationships work well, while others may struggle. One of the key insights to be gained from the law of gender is the understanding that we cannot change others, only ourselves. This is because we each have our own unique energy and vibration that shape our perceptions and experiences. When we try to change others, we are essentially trying to change their energy and vibration, which is not only impossible but also counterproductive. Instead, we must focus on changing ourselves, recognizing that when we do so, we change the dynamic of our relationships and create a more harmonious and fulfilling experience.

Forgiveness is a necessary step in this process of change, as it allows us to release any negative emotions or resentment we may be holding onto toward others. Forgiveness is not about excusing bad behavior or letting others off the hook, but rather, it's about releasing the emotional hold that someone or something has over us. This can be a difficult step to take, but it's essential to our growth and well-being.

When we forgive, we release the burden of negative emotions, and we open ourselves up to a brighter future.

The law of gender and forgiveness are two concepts that are intertwined and have a powerful impact on our lives. Understanding the law of gender helps us to appreciate the unique energy and vibration that each person brings to our lives, while forgiveness allows us to release negative emotions and create a more harmonious experience. By appreciating these laws and putting them into practice, we can improve our relationships and build a more fulfilling life.

Takeaways and tips. When it comes to the Law of Gender and Forgiveness, there are several practical tips that can help you put these concepts into action.

1. Practice Self-Awareness: To understand the law of gender, you must first become aware of your own energy and vibration. Take some time each day to reflect on your thoughts, feelings, and actions. This self-awareness will help you understand how your energy affects your relationships and help you identify areas where you can make changes.

2. Embrace your Masculine and Feminine Energy: The law of gender recognizes that others are essentially trying to control them, which is not only impossible but also counterproductive. Instead, take responsibility for your thoughts and actions. This will help you build stronger relationships based on mutual respect and understanding.

3. Practice Forgiveness: Forgiveness is not just a one-time event, but a daily practice. Take time each day to release any negative emotions or resentment you may be holding onto. This will help you create a more positive outlook on life and build stronger relationships.

4. Focus on the Present Moment: To put the law of gender into action, you must focus on the present moment. Don't dwell on the past or worry about the future. Instead, focus on what's happening right now, and pay attention to how your energy affects those around you.

5. Take responsibility for Your Thoughts and Actions

In conclusion, these tips are just the beginning of what you can do to put the Law of Gender and Forgiveness into action. By following these tips and practicing these concepts, you can improve your relationships, build a more fulfilling life, and become a more harmonious and happier person.

Both masculine and feminine energies are important and necessary for a harmonious relationship. Embrace both aspects of yourself and strive to create a balance between your masculine and feminine energies. This balance will help you create a more fulfilling life and stronger relationships.

Chapter 13:
The Power of Forgiveness

"Forgive to Live: The Key to Unlocking
Unlimited Joy!"

Forgiveness is a powerful and transformative
tool that has the ability to free us from the
chains of anger, resentment, and bitterness that
hold us back from living a full and fulfilling life.
At the core of this is the relationship between a
lack of love and a lack of forgiveness, which
can often go hand in hand.

When we don't love ourselves, we struggle to extend love and compassion to others, and this lack of love can easily translate into a lack of forgiveness.

To truly understand the power of forgiveness, it is essential to look within ourselves and identify the areas where forgiveness is required. This can be a difficult and challenging process, as it involves facing the pain and hurt that we have experienced, both from others and ourselves. However, it is only by looking within and acknowledging these wounds that we can begin to heal and move forward.

Forgiving others is an important step in the journey towards self-love and healing. This involves letting go of anger, resentment, and bitterness, and replacing them with understanding, compassion, and a willingness to see the situation from the other person's perspective. It is important to remember that forgiving someone does not mean that you condone their actions, or that you are letting them off the hook for what they have done. Rather, it means that you are freeing yourself from the negative energy that has been holding you back.

Forgiving oneself is equally important, as we often carry a heavy burden of self-blame and self-criticism that can weigh us down.

This self-forgiveness involves acknowledging our own mistakes and shortcomings and offering ourselves the same understanding and compassion that we extend to others.

The release of energy that follows forgiveness is nothing short of miraculous. It is as if a heavy weight has been lifted from our shoulders, allowing us to move forward with a renewed sense of purpose and vitality. The sense of peace and joy that comes from forgiving others and oneself is truly life-changing, and the impact it has on our relationships and our overall well-being is immeasurable.

The power of forgiveness lies in its ability to break the cycle of lack of love and lack of forgiveness that can hold us back from living a full and fulfilling life. By looking within, forgiving others and oneself and releasing the negative energy that has been holding us back, we can find peace, joy, and a renewed sense of purpose. So, take the first step today, and discover the transformative power of forgiveness for yourself!

Here are some tips for harnessing its transformative energy in your own life.

1. Be honest with yourself. The first step in the journey of forgiveness is to be honest with yourself about the areas where forgiveness is required. Take a deep look within, and acknowledge any pain, hurt, or resentment that you may be holding onto. Remember, this is a brave and courageous step, and you deserve to be gentle with yourself as you navigate this process.

2. Practice empathy. To forgive others, it is essential to practice empathy and try to see the situation from their perspective. This does not mean that you condone their actions, but it does help to break down the barriers of anger and resentment that can prevent you from extending forgiveness.

3. Let go of perfectionism. Forgiving oneself is often more challenging than forgiving others, as we tend to be our own harshest critics. However, it is important to let go of the perfectionism that can prevent us from forgiving ourselves. Remember that we are all human, and we all make mistakes. Offer yourself the same understanding and compassion that you would extend to a friend.

4. Focus on the present. Forgiveness is a process that takes time, and it can be tempting to dwell on the past or worry about the future. However, the key to finding peace and joy through forgiveness is to focus on the present moment. Take each step one day at a time, and trust in the journey.

5. Surround yourself with support. Forgiveness can be a challenging journey, but you don't have to go it alone. Surround yourself with supportive friends and family and reach out for help if you need it. Whether it's through therapy, support groups, or simply talking to a trusted friend, connecting with others can provide the encouragement and strength you need to keep moving forward.

In conclusion, the tips I have shared are just the beginning of your journey towards the power of forgiveness. Remember to be honest with yourself, practice empathy, let go of perfectionism, focus on the present, and surround yourself with support. With these tools in your toolbox, you will find the strength and courage to forgive, heal, and live a life filled with love and joy. So, go ahead, take the first step today, and discover the transformative power of forgiveness.

Chapter 14:
The Law of Vibration

"Your thoughts, your energy, your life: Master
the Law of Vibration."

The Law of Vibration is a universal principle
that states everything in the universe is
constantly vibrating and in motion. This includes
our thoughts, emotions, and physical bodies,
which are all made up of energy that is
constantly vibrating at different frequencies.

The concept of the Law of Vibration is based on the idea that like attracts like meaning that our thoughts, emotions, and physical bodies will attract similar vibrations to themselves.

One of the most significant ways that the Law of Vibration affects our lives is through its impact on our health and well-being. Our physical bodies are highly sensitive to the energy that surrounds us, and they respond to this energy in various ways. When we are feeling happy and positive, our energy vibrates at a higher frequency, which can lead to better health, more energy, and a greater sense of well-being. On the other hand, when we are feeling negative or stressed, our energy vibrates at a lower frequency, which can lead to physical and mental health issues.

A great example of how the Law of Vibration can impact our health and well-being is the story of Norman Cousins, an American journalist and political commentator who used humor and laughter to help him recover from a severe illness. Norman was diagnosed with a life-threatening autoimmune disease, and he was told that he had only a few months to live. Instead of resigning himself to his fate, he decided to take control of his health by using laughter as a tool for healing. He watched funny movies, read humorous books, and surrounded himself with people who made him laugh.

To his surprise, he found that laughter had a profound impact on his energy levels and physical well-being, and he eventually made a full recovery.

The story of Norman Cousins highlights the importance of not taking ourselves too seriously and the impact that breaking out of mental prisons can have on our health and well-being. When we can find humor and joy in life, we can raise our energy vibration, which can lead to better health, more energy, and a greater sense of well-being. The Law of Vibration reminds us that we have the power to control our thoughts, emotions, and physical bodies and that by doing so, we can create a life filled with health, happiness, and success.

Here are some tips and takeaways from this chapter to help you harness the power of this universal principle and create a life filled with health, happiness, and success:

1. Be aware of your thoughts: Our thoughts are powerful, and they are significant so, it is essential to be aware as they have an impact on the energy that surrounds us. By becoming aware of your thoughts, you can begin to change them to more positive, uplifting ones. This can help raise your energy vibration and improve your overall health and well-being.

2. Practice gratitude: Gratitude is one of the most powerful ways to raise your energy vibration. When you focus on the things in your life that you are grateful for, you are sending out a positive energy that attracts more positivity and abundance into your life.

3. Surround yourself with positive energy: The people you surround yourself with have a significant impact on your energy vibration. Try to surround yourself with positive, uplifting people who make you feel good and inspire you to be your best self.

4. Laugh and have fun: Laughter and fun are powerful tools for raising your energy vibration. Make time for activities that bring you joy, and try to find humor in the situations you find yourself in.

5. Take care of your physical body: Your physical body is highly sensitive to energy,

By following these tips, you can harness the power of the Law of Vibration and create a life filled with health, happiness, and success. Just remember to have fun, laugh often, and keep a positive outlook, and you'll be amazed at what you can achieve.

Chapter 15:

Complementing Exercise with Other Aspects of Life

"Balance your life, align your vibration, live your best life."

The topic of balancing various aspects of life with exercise and nutrition is a crucial one for overall health and energy. It's a well-known fact that exercise and a nutritious diet are important for a healthy lifestyle, but what often gets overlooked is the importance of balancing these things with other aspects of life, such as relationships, finances, and family.

We live in a fast-paced world, and it can be easy to get caught up in the hustle and bustle of daily life, leaving us feeling drained and burnt out. This is why it's essential to make time for the things that matter most, such as spending time with loved ones, managing our finances, and taking care of our health.

But did you know that it's not just our physical actions that affect our health, but our thoughts and attitudes as well? It's true! Our thoughts and attitudes play a significant role in determining the vibratory rate of our body, and this rate can either support or sabotage our efforts to maintain good health.

This is where affirmations come in.

Affirmations are positive statements that help align our thoughts and attitudes with the laws of vibration. By repeating affirmations, we can shift our focus from negative thoughts to positive ones, which can in turn help raise our vibratory rate and increase our energy levels.

For example, instead of thinking "I'm too busy to exercise," try saying, "I make time for exercise because it's important for my health." This simple shift in thought patterns can help you feel more motivated and energized to make exercise a priority in your life.

Balancing relationships, finances, and family with exercise and nutrition is crucial for overall health and energy. But it's also important to pay attention to our thought patterns and attitudes, as they can either support or sabotage our efforts to maintain good health.

By using affirmations, we can align our thoughts and attitudes with the law of vibration, helping us feel more energized and motivated to live a healthy, balanced life.

Regarding the importance of balancing relationships, finances, and family with exercise and nutrition for overall health and energy, here are some tips and takeaways.

1. Make a schedule and stick to it: One of the best ways to balance multiple aspects of life is to create a schedule and stick to it. This way, you can allocate time for exercise, family, work, and other important tasks, making sure you don't overlook any of them.

2. Prioritize self-care: It's important to prioritize self-care and make time for yourself. Whether it's taking a relaxing bath, reading a book, or going for a walk, make sure to set aside some time each day to do something that makes you happy.

3. Practice mindfulness: Mindfulness is a powerful tool for reducing stress and promoting balance in your life. Try to take a few minutes each day to focus on your breathing and clear your mind of any negative thoughts.

4. Surround yourself with positive people: The people you surround yourself with can have a huge impact on your thoughts and attitudes. Try to surround yourself with positive, supportive individuals who will encourage you on your journey towards a healthier, more balanced life.

5. Use affirmations: As mentioned in the previous answer, affirmations can be a powerful tool for aligning your thoughts and attitudes with the law of vibration. Try repeating positive affirmations each day to help boost your energy levels and maintain a positive outlook.

6. Celebrate small victories: Finally, it's important to celebrate your progress, no matter how small it may be. Whether it's completing a workout or making a healthy meal, acknowledge and celebrate your efforts towards a healthier, more balanced life.

In conclusion, balancing relationships, finances and family with exercise and nutrition for overall health and energy requires effort and dedication, but it's definitely worth it! By following these tips, you can improve your vibratory rate, increase your energy levels, and live a healthier, more balanced life.

Chapter 16:
The Power of Health and Strength

"Elevate Your Life: Balance Exercise and Nutrition with Purpose."

Health and strength are two of the most powerful elements that define our existence. They hold the key to unlocking our full potential and living a life that is full of meaning and purpose. In today's world, where stress and unhealthy habits are rampant, it's more important than ever to take control of our bodies and create a healing environment within.

At the heart of this transformative power lies the idea that we are in control of our own bodies. We have the power to shape and mold it into whatever we desire. But to do this, we must first understand the law of gender. This law states that everything in the universe has a male and female aspect, and we must balance these aspects within ourselves to achieve true health and strength. The same goes for our relationships.

Forgiveness is key to maintaining balance and harmony, not only in our relationships but also within ourselves.

The law of vibration is another critical concept to understand. This law states that everything in the universe vibrates at a specific frequency and that our thoughts and emotions also vibrate. The more positive our thoughts and emotions are, the higher our frequency will be, which will attract more positivity into our lives. On the other hand, negative thoughts and emotions lower our frequency and attract negativity.

This is why affirmations are such a powerful tool for aligning with the law of vibration and creating a healing environment within.

Exercise and nutrition are two critical components of health and strength, but it's important to balance these with other aspects of our lives. This includes our relationships, work, and spiritual pursuits.

Only by balancing all these aspects can we truly achieve optimal health and strength.

Ultimately, the message is that health and strength lie within each of us. It's up to us to decide to create a healing environment within our bodies and live the life we truly desire. By embracing the transformative power of health and strength, we can become our best selves and live a life filled with purpose, happiness, and success. So, let's embrace this power and create the lives we deserve!

It's not just about having a fit and toned body, but it's about creating a healing environment within and embracing the transformative power that comes with it. So, without further ado.

Here are some tips that I've found to be crucial in harnessing this power:

1. Embrace the law of gender: Understanding the balance of male and female energies within ourselves is key to unlocking our full potential. Seek to balance these aspects in all areas of your life, including your relationships, work, and spirituality.

2. Forgive and let go: Holding onto grudges and resentment only hinders our growth and success. Forgiveness is a powerful tool for maintaining balance and harmony in our lives. It's not about forgetting or excusing hurtful behavior, but rather letting go of the emotional charge it holds over us.

3. Align with the law of vibration: Our thoughts and emotions vibrate at a specific frequency, and it's up to us to ensure that this frequency is high and positive.

   Affirmations are a great way to do this.

   Repeat positive affirmations throughout the day to align with the law of vibration and attract positivity into your life.

4. Balance exercise and nutrition with other aspects of life: It's important to strike a balance between exercise and nutrition, but it's equally important to balance these with other aspects of life, such as relationships, work, and spiritual pursuits. Achieving a holistic balance will lead to optimal health and strength.

5. Practice self-care: Taking care of yourself is key to creating a healing environment within. Incorporate activities that bring you joy and peace, such as reading, meditating, or spending time in nature.

6. Embrace the power within: Remember that the power of health and strength lies within each of us. It's up to us to decide to create a healing environment and embrace the transformative power that comes with it.

By incorporating these tips into your daily life, you too can harness the power of health and strength and become your best self. So, what are you waiting for? Embrace the transformative power within and live the life you truly deserve!

Chapter 17:

Forgiving and Releasing Negative Emotions

"Release the pain and open the door to a peaceful life."

Forgiving and releasing negative emotions is one of the most crucial practices for a healthy and fulfilling life. It is a journey that requires deep introspection, self-awareness, and a commitment to personal growth and well-being. At the heart of this process lies the concept of forgiveness, both of oneself and others.

Forgiveness is not simply a matter of letting go of anger or resentment. It is a profound act of love and compassion, a recognition that we are all human and that we all make mistakes.

When we hold onto negative emotions like resentment, stress, fear, doubt, and others, we create an inner environment that is toxic and damaging to our health and happiness. These emotions take up valuable space in our minds and hearts, and they can interfere with our ability to live life to the fullest. They can cause us to feel anxious, stressed, or even physically ill.

However, when we practice forgiveness and release these emotions, we open the door to a more peaceful and joyful life. One of the most effective ways to release negative emotions is through meditation.

Meditation allows us to quiet our minds and focus on the present moment, which can help us gain perspective on our thoughts and emotions.

When we meditate, we also activate the parasympathetic nervous system, which is responsible for calming and relaxing the body. This can help us feel more relaxed and at peace, even in the face of challenging circumstances.

In addition to meditation, it is important to do the things that bring us joy and align us with our spirit. This can be anything from spending time in nature, practicing a hobby, or connecting with loved ones. Doing things that bring us joy can help us feel more connected to our sense of purpose and can also help us let go of negative emotions more easily.

Visualization is another powerful tool for releasing negative emotions. One visualization technique involves imagining beautiful lavender energy flowing into your body. Lavender is associated with peace, tranquility, and calm, so visualizing this energy can help you feel more relaxed and at peace. Imagine this energy entering your body and flowing through every cell, vibrating in harmony with God's laws. As you visualize this, feel yourself becoming more and more relaxed, and imagine any negative emotions flowing out of your body and being replaced by peace and love.

Forgiving and releasing negative emotions is a critical step on the path to personal growth and well-being. By practicing forgiveness, meditating, doing things that bring us joy, and visualizing positive energy, we can transform our lives and live with greater peace and happiness. So, take some time today to forgive yourself and others, release any negative emotions that are holding you back, and embrace the beauty and wonder of life.

Here are some tips for practicing forgiveness and releasing negative emotions: Embrace self-awareness:

1. The first step in releasing negative emotions is to understand and acknowledge what emotions you are holding onto. Take some time each day to reflect on your thoughts and feelings and be honest with yourself about what emotions are holding you back.

2. Practice mindfulness: Mindfulness is a powerful tool for releasing negative emotions. It involves paying attention to your thoughts and feelings in the present moment without judgment. By practicing mindfulness, you can become more aware of your emotions and gain a new perspective on your life.

3. Forgive yourself: Forgiving yourself is just as important as forgiving others. Take some time to reflect on your past mistakes and forgive yourself for any wrongdoings. Remember that we all make mistakes and that forgiving yourself is a sign of strength and resilience.

4. Forgive others: Forgiving others is not about condoning their actions, but rather it's about letting go of anger and resentment so that you can move forward with a sense of peace and happiness.

5. Let go of grudges and focus on the positive aspects of your relationships.

6. Connect with nature: Spending time in nature can be incredibly healing and grounding. Take a walk in the park, go for a hike, or simply sit outside and observe the beauty of nature. Connecting with the natural world can help you release negative emotions and feel more connected to the world around you.

7. Practice gratitude: Gratitude is a powerful tool for releasing negative emotions and promoting well-being. Make a habit of listing things you're grateful for each day, no matter how small they may seem. This practice can help you shift your focus from what's wrong in your life to what's right.

8. Laugh and have fun: Laughter is one of the best medicines for releasing negative emotions. So, make time for activities that bring you joy and laughter, like watching a comedy, playing with friends, or simply having a good time.

9. Visualize positive energy: A visualization is a powerful tool for releasing negative emotions. Close your eyes and imagine a beautiful light, such as lavender energy, flowing into your body and filling you with peace and happiness.

10. Visualize all your cells vibrating in
    harmony with God's laws and imagine any
    negative emotions leaving your body.

In conclusion, practicing forgiveness and releasing negative emotions is a journey that requires time, effort, and a commitment to personal growth. By embracing self-awareness, practicing mindfulness, forgiving yourself and others, connecting with nature, practicing gratitude, laughing, and visualizing positive energy, you can transform your life and live with greater peace and happiness.

Chapter 18:

Staying in the Moment and Focusing on the Good

"Focus on the Good and Reap the Rewards"

Staying in the moment and focusing on the good is an incredibly important way to maintain our power, both mentally and emotionally. It's a great reminder to stay grounded and connected to the present moment and to be mindful of how we feel and how our actions impact our lives.

Rather than dwelling on the negative, or worrying about the future, we can instead stay in the moment and focus on the good. This helps us to appreciate the present moment and to recognize the beauty of the world around us. When we pay attention to the present, we can take the time to appreciate our successes and learn from our mistakes. Having dreams and aspirations can also help us stay in the moment and focus on the good.

Focusing on our goals and having an idea of where we want to go can give us a sense of purpose and direction. We can use our dreams and aspirations to motivate us to keep pushing forward, no matter how difficult the situation may be. It's also important to remember to focus on the good side of the situation. We all have bad days, but if we take the time to focus on the positive aspects of our lives, we can keep our spirits up and be stronger and healthier each day. This can mean blessings, recognizing our strengths, or simply finding joy in the small moments.

By staying in the moment and focusing on the good, we can maintain our power and keep growing. We can keep our minds and hearts open and appreciate the beauty of the present moment. We can use our dreams and aspirations to propel us forward and recognize the positive aspects of our lives.

Finally, we can repeat this mantra to ourselves each day and get healthier and stronger each day.

Here are some tips for staying in the moment and focusing on the good.

1. Remember to take a few moments each day to stay in the moment and focus on the good. This could mean taking a few deep breaths or simply appreciating the beauty of the world around you.

2. Make sure to set realistic goals and aspirations. This will help to motivate you to move forward and stay motivated.

3. Find joy in the small moments. This could mean taking time to appreciate a beautiful sunset or taking a few moments to appreciate the blessings in your life.

4. Recognize your strengths. Take time to recognize the things that you are good at and use them to stay motivated.

5. Take a few moments each day to remind yourself of the mantra "Stay in the moment and focus on the good." This will help to keep you grounded and connected to the present moment.

6. Keep your mind and heart open. This will help to keep a healthy perspective and allow you to take in the beauty of the world around you.

7. Finally, take time to appreciate the successes in your life. This will give you a sense of accomplishment and help you to stay positive.

Chapter 19:

Finding and Expressing Your Life Purpose

"Live life with purpose and intention - Unlock your potential"

Living your life with purpose and intention is something that each and every one of us should strive for. Our life purpose can be found through deep introspection and self- exploration. It's important to take time to reflect on the values, beliefs, and passions that drive us. Once we have a clear idea of our purpose, it's important to express it outwardly.

We should strive to live our lives in alignment with our purpose and act in accordance with the values and beliefs we stand for. One of the most impactful ways to express our life purpose is through our actions. Taking action toward our goals and dreams is key to fulfilling our purpose. We should strive to make every effort to bring our dreams to life. Whether it's starting a business, writing a book, or helping others, it's important to take action in areas that are in line with our purpose.

Another way to express our life purpose is through our words. We should use our words to inspire, motivate, and empower those around us.

Whether it's through speaking, writing, or even social media, our words can have a big impact on those around us. We should use our words to share our passion and continue to spread positivity and light.

Finally, we can express our life purpose through our presence. We should strive to be present and mindful in our interactions with others. We should use our presence and energy to uplift and encourage those around us. Our presence and energy can be

powerful tools to help others discover and unlock their true potential. Living with purpose is a powerful way to make an impact on the world.

By taking time to reflect on our values, beliefs, and passions, we can discover our life's purpose and use it to guide us in our lives. We can express our life purpose through our actions, words, and presence and use it to make a positive impact on our lives and the lives of those around us. To strive to live our lives with purpose and intention and make an impact on the world.

Here are some tips for finding and expressing your life purpose.

1. Take time to reflect: In order to find our life purpose, it's important to take time to reflect on our values and beliefs. We should focus on what brings us joy, contentment, and fulfillment.

2. Take action: Once we've found our purpose, it's important to take action and strive to bring our dreams to life. We should focus on taking action steps that are in line with our purpose.

3. Use our words: Our words have power and can be used to empower and motivate those around us. We should use our words to share our passion and spread positivity and light.

4. Be present: Our presence and energy can be powerful tools to help others discover and unlock their true potential. We should strive to be mindful and present in our interactions with others.

5. Make an impact: Living with purpose is a powerful way to make an impact on the world. We should use our purpose to guide our lives and use it to make a positive impact on our lives and the lives of those around us.

6. Take time to reflect: In order to find our life purpose, it's important to take time to reflect on our values and beliefs. We should focus on what brings us joy, contentment, and fulfillment.

7. Take action: Once we've found our purpose, it's important to take action and strive to bring our dreams to life. We should focus on taking action steps that are in line with our purpose.

8. Use our words: Our words have power and can be used to empower and motivate those around us. We should use our words to share our passion and spread positivity and light.

9. Be present: Our presence and energy can be powerful tools to help others discover and unlock their true potential. We should strive to be mindful and present in our interactions with others.

10. Make an impact: Living with purpose is a powerful way to make an impact on the world. We should use our purpose to guide our lives and use it to make a positive impact on our lives and the lives of those around us.

Chapter 20:

The Law of Polarity and the Present Moment

"Let go of the past, embrace the present: live an epic life.

When we focus our attention on the present moment, we become aware of the polarities that exist within us and around us. We see the balance between our thoughts, emotions, and physical sensations. We understand the interconnections between our actions and the impact they have on others and the world. We have the power to choose how we want to respond to these polarities – whether we want to move towards more light, more love, or more peace. This is why the present moment is so important – it is where we have the opportunity to shape our reality and create the life we want to live. When we focus on the present moment, we

can tap into our own inner wisdom, creativity, and power. We can learn to respond to the polarities in our lives with grace, wisdom, and compassion.

I invite you to embrace the law of polarity and the power of the present moment. Let us choose to live in the now, and to create a world that is balanced, harmonious, and full of love. After all, that is the true path to happiness, fulfillment, and a life well-lived.

Here are some takeaways from this chapter and my favorite ways to tap into the power of the now and live a more balanced and fulfilling life:

1. Practice mindfulness: The first step to living in the present moment is to practice mindfulness. This means paying attention to your thoughts, emotions, and physical sensations, and learning to observe them without judgment. You can start by taking a few minutes each day to simply sit still and focus on your breath. Over time, you'll find that mindfulness becomes easier and more natural, and you'll be able to bring this awareness into your daily life.

2. Cultivate gratitude: Another way to tap into the power of the present moment is to cultivate a daily practice of gratitude. When we focus on what we have, rather than what we don't have, we create a positive and balanced perspective on life. You can start by writing down three things you're grateful for each day, or simply taking a few moments to appreciate the good things in your life.

3. Find balance: The law of polarity reminds us that everything exists in relationship to something else. To live a balanced life, we need to find a balance between the different aspects of our lives – work, play, relationships, and self-care. Take a step back, assess where you're spending your time and energy, and make adjustments as needed to create a more harmonious balance.

4. Embrace change: Change is an inevitable part of life, but it can also be a source of anxiety and stress. The law of polarity teaches us that everything exists in relation to something else, and that change is simply the movement from one polarity to another. Embracing change means learning to let go of what no longer serves us and moving towards what does.

5. Live in the present: Finally, the most important tip I can offer is to simply live in the present moment. When we're living in the now, we're tapping into the power of the present moment and connecting with our true selves. This means letting go of regrets about the past and worries about the future and focusing on what's happening right now.

By embracing the law of polarity and the present moment, you'll find that life becomes more balanced, harmonious, and fulfilling. So, my dear reader, I hope these tips help you tap into the power of the now and live your best life!

Chapter 21:

Happiness as a Process

"Discover your happiness: A journey to self-discovery."

Happiness is a journey, not a destination. It is something that we must constantly work on, not simply a box that we tick off our list of life accomplishments. We must strive to understand who we are, what we love, and what truly makes us happy. The pursuit of happiness is a lifetime endeavor and not a one-time event.

The pursuit of happiness begins with self-discovery. Who are we, what do we value, what do we stand for, and what do we love to do? When we know these things about ourselves, we can better understand what will bring us joy and fulfillment. This requires introspection and honest self-reflection. It requires us to look within ourselves and ask difficult questions about what truly drives us.

Next, we must strive for satisfaction in our lives and not just the pursuit of money. While money is an important factor in life, it should not be the sole driving force behind our pursuits.

We must find joy and fulfillment in the work that we do. Whether it's through our careers, hobbies, or volunteer work, when we find satisfaction in what we do, we can experience a deep sense of happiness and contentment.

Finally, it's important to focus on the good qualities in ourselves and others. Too often, we get caught up in being judgmental and critical of others, or even of ourselves. This negative outlook can bring us down and dampen our spirit. Instead, we must learn to focus on the positive aspects of our lives and those around us. We must seek to appreciate the good in others and ourselves, even in the face of challenges and obstacles.

Happiness is a process, not a destination. We must work towards it, every day, by striving for self-discovery, satisfaction, and a positive outlook. When we do these things, we can experience a sense of joy, fulfillment, and contentment that lasts a lifetime. So, let us embark on this journey of happiness, with open hearts and minds, and a willingness to grow, learn, and evolve as we go.

If you're looking to make happiness a part of your everyday life, here are some tips and to help you get started on your journey:

1. Prioritize satisfaction over money: Yes, money is important, but it shouldn't be the only factor driving your decisions. Find work that you love, hobbies that bring you joy, and volunteering for causes that are meaningful to you.

2. Get to know yourself: Take the time to reflect on who you are, what you stand for, and what brings you joy. This self-discovery will be the foundation for everything else you do in your pursuit of happiness.

3. Surround yourself with positivity: Seek out positive people and environments. Surrounding yourself with positive energy will help lift your spirits and bring a sense of happiness to your life.

4. Practice gratitude: Make a habit of focusing on the things you're thankful for. When you focus on the good in your life, it's easier to find happiness and contentment.

5. Let go of judgment: Don't spend your time and energy being critical of yourself or others. Instead, focus on the good in everyone and everything.

6. Embrace change: Life is full of change, and it can be scary, but it can also bring new opportunities and experiences that can bring happiness and fulfillment.

7. Cultivate kindness: Be kind to yourself and others. When you practice kindness, you'll experience a sense of happiness and well-being that comes from doing good for others.

8. Find balance: It's important to have a balance of work, play, and rest. When you strike the right balance, you'll feel more energized, productive, and happy.

By following these tips, you'll be well on your way to making happiness a part of your daily life. Remember, happiness is a process, not a destination. It requires effort, rejection, and a positive outlook. So, embrace the journey and enjoy the ride!

Chapter 22:

Pursuing Dreams and Overcoming Fears

"Turn failures into opportunities, chase your dreams with passion."

Pursuing your dreams and overcoming fears is a journey like no other. It's a test of our willpower, determination, and perseverance. Fear of failure and success can both hold us back, but it's crucial that we push past these fears and chase our aspirations with all we've got.

Failure and success are two sides of the same coin, and both are necessary for growth.

Failure teaches us valuable lessons that success never could. It shows us what we need to work on, where our weaknesses lie, and how to be better next time. It helps us build resilience and determination and makes us stronger. Without failure, success would mean nothing.

However, fear of failure can be debilitating. It can prevent us from even trying, from putting ourselves out there, from taking that first step. But it's important to understand that failure is not the end. It's not a sign of defeat but of progress. Every failure is an opportunity to learn, grow, and become better.

Fear of success can be just as damaging. It's the fear of the unknown, of change, of being vulnerable. We might worry that success will come with its own set of challenges and responsibilities, that will alter our lives in ways we're not prepared for. But success is not something to be feared, it's something to be embraced.

Success brings new opportunities, new connections, and new experiences. It can help us fulfill our potential and make a positive impact on the world. But it's also important to remember that success is not a destination, it's a journey.

There will always be new challenges and obstacles, but as long as we continue to pursue our dreams and overcome our fears, success will be within our reach.

Pursuing your dreams and overcoming fears is a journey worth taking. Fear of failure and success can be crippling, but we must push past these fears and chase our aspirations with all we've got. Embrace failure, as it will teach us more than success ever could, and embrace success, as it brings new opportunities, experiences, and fulfillment.

Here are some tips to help you along the way:

1. Embrace failure: Don't be afraid of failure. Embrace it, learn from it, and use it to your advantage. Every failure is an opportunity to grow and become better.

2. Celebrate small wins: Celebrating your small wins along the way will help keep you motivated and on track. Celebrate each accomplishment, no matter how small, and acknowledge the progress you've made.

3. Focus on the journey, not just the destination: Pursuing your dreams is not just about reaching the finish line, but about the journey along the way. Focus on the progress you're making, the experiences you're having, and the person you're becoming.

4. Surround yourself with positivity:
Surround yourself with positive people
who support your dreams and encourage
you to keep going. Being around
negative people can be detrimental to your
journey, so make sure you surround
yourself with positivity.

5. Believe in yourself: Believe in yourself
and your abilities. Trust in your instincts,
and don't let fear hold you back. Believe
that you're capable of accomplishing
your
dreams and overcoming any obstacles in
your path.

6. Take action: Taking action is key to
pursuing your dreams. Don't wait for the
perfect opportunity or for everything to be
just right. Take the first step and keep
moving forward, no matter how small the
steps may be.

7. Stay focused: Stay focused on your goals
and don't let distractions pull you away.
Keep your eyes on the prize, and don't let
fear or doubt stand in your way.

In conclusion, pursuing your dreams and
overcoming fears requires courage,
determination, and the right mindset.
Embrace failure, celebrate small wins, focus on
the journey, surround yourself with positivity,
believe in yourself, take action, and stay
focused. With these tips in mind, you'll be on
your way to chasing your dreams and realizing
your full potential.

Chapter 23:

Creating or Disintegrating

"Create the future, shape your legacy."

Creating or disintegrating, these two actions
form the core of what it means to be human.
They represent the fundamental choice that
we make every moment of every day, whether
we are conscious of it or not. To create is to
build, to shape, to bring into existence
something that was not there before.

To disintegrate is to break down, to destroy, to reduce to nothing what was once there. These actions are not limited to physical things like buildings and bridges, they also apply to ideas, relationships, and our own sense of self

Creating is a powerful force. It is the driving force behind progress, behind every discovery, and every act of kindness. It requires a clear goal, a plan, and most importantly, action. It requires us to focus on what we want to bring into the world and to put our hearts and minds into making it a reality. This is not always an easy task, but the reward of creating is immeasurable. Whether it is a work of art, a business, a relationship, or simply a new way of thinking, the act of creation brings joy, purpose, and meaning to our lives. Disintegrating, on the other hand, is a destructive force. It can be tempting to focus on tearing down what we don't like, what we don't understand, or what stands in our way. But this is a limited and ultimately self-defeating perspective. Disintegrating without purpose, without thought, and without caring for the consequences is a recipe for disaster. It can lead to a loss of trust, a lack of cooperation, and a world that is less safe and less secure.

The meta secret of life, then, is to understand that we have a choice in every moment. We can choose to create or disintegrate. The key is to focus on others' benefits, not just our own.

When we approach our lives with a focus on creating value for those around us, we are more likely to find happiness, success, and fulfillment. We are more likely to build meaningful relationships, contribute to our communities, and make a positive impact on the world.

So, let us embrace the power of creation and choose to focus on building and shaping the world around us. Let us bring our unique talents, passions, and perspectives to the table and work together to create a world that is better for everyone.

Whether it is through our words, our actions, or our ideas, let us leave a positive legacy that will endure long after we are gone.

The choice is ours; the opportunity is ours, and the future is ours to create.

To help you embrace the power of creation, here are some tips that will inspire and guide you on your journey.

1. Set a clear goal: The first step to creating something new is to have a clear vision of what you want to achieve. What are you passionate about? What do you want to build or create? Having a clear goal will help you stay focused and motivated as you work towards it.

2. Make a plan: Once you have your goal in mind, it's time to create a plan of action. What steps will you need to take to get there? Who will you need to collaborate with? What resources will you need? Having a plan will help you stay organized and on track.

3. Take action: The most important step in the process of creation is taking action. Ideas and plans are great, but they won't do you any good unless you take the leap and start working toward your goal. So, get started, take that first step, and keep moving forward.

4. Focus on others' benefits: One of the keys to creating something truly great is to focus on how it will benefit others. Whether it's a new business, a community project, or a new way of thinking, ask yourself how you can make a positive impact on the world.

5. Embrace collaboration: Creation is rarely a one-person effort. Whether it's working with a team, seeking feedback, or seeking help when you need it, embracing collaboration will help you create something that is greater than the sum of its parts.

6. Stay positive: Finally, it's important to stay positive, and optimistic, even when things get tough. Remember why you started, stay focused on your goal, and keep moving forward. With hard work and determination, you can achieve anything you set your mind to.

In conclusion, by following these tips, you can embrace the power of creation and make a positive impact on the world. Whether it's through your work, your relationships, or your ideas, you have the power to shape the future and leave a legacy that will endure for generations to come. So go ahead, choose to create, and make your mark on the world.

Chapter 24:
Embracing Abundance and Joy

"Celebrate your wins and live life to the fullest."

At the heart of it all, we each have everything
we need to achieve our purpose, to be happy,
and to find joy in our journey. So, how can we
tap into this inner wellspring of abundance?

First, it's essential to love and appreciate who
we are. When we do this, we radiate a positive
energy that attracts others and good things into
our lives.

It's important to remember that we are unique, special, and deserving of happiness. By embracing our individuality and embracing our strengths and weaknesses, we open the door to true self-acceptance.

Second, we must appreciate the grand miracle of life itself. When we pause to consider the complexity and beauty of the universe and our place within it, it's easy to feel overwhelmed by a sense of awe and wonder. Every sunrise, every sunset, every moment in between is a blessing, and it's up to us to make the most of each one.

Third, it's crucial to love and appreciate those around us. Whether it's family, friends, or even strangers, each person we encounter is here for a reason.

By embracing them with open hearts and minds, we create a sense of community and support that strengthens and uplifts us all.

Finally, by embracing abundance and joy, we cultivate a positive outlook on life. We become more confident, optimistic, and resilient, even in the face of adversity. When we focus on the good, we attract good into our lives, and the cycle of positivity continues.

Embracing abundance and joy is a simple yet profound way to live a fulfilling life.

By loving ourselves, appreciating the miracle of life, embracing those around us, and cultivating a positive outlook, we open the door to a world of happiness, abundance, and purpose.

Here are some techniques that have worked for me, and I'm confident they'll work for you too. So, let's dive in!

1. Practice gratitude: Gratitude is a powerful tool that can help us shift our focus from what's wrong in our lives to what's right. Each day, take a moment to reflect on the things you're thankful for, no matter how small they may seem. This simple practice will help you cultivate a sense of abundance and joy that permeates every aspect of your life.

2. Embrace self-care: Self-care is essential to our well-being, both physically and mentally. When we take care of ourselves, we feel better, and when we feel better, we're better equipped to handle life's challenges. So, make time for the things that nourish you, whether it's a bubble bath, a yoga class, or a quiet walk in the park.

3. Connect with nature: Nature has a way of restoring our spirits and helping us find peace.

4. Whether it's a hike in the woods, a picnic in the park, or simply sitting on a bench and taking in the sights and sounds of the world around you, connecting with nature is an excellent way to tap into a sense of abundance and joy.

5. Surround yourself with positivity: The people we surround ourselves with have a profound impact on our well-being. So, make an effort to spend time with people who bring out the best in you, and distance yourself from those who bring you down. By filling your life with positive energy, you'll find that abundance and joy come more easily.

6. Celebrate your wins: No matter how small they may seem, it's important to acknowledge and celebrate your successes. Doing so helps to build self-confidence and reinforces a sense of abundance and joy. So, keep a tally of your wins, big and small, and take time to celebrate each one.

In conclusion, these tips are just the beginning when it comes to embracing abundance and joy. By incorporating them into your daily life, you'll be well on your way to a life-filled with purpose, happiness, and fulfillment. So, don't wait, start embracing abundance and joy today!

Chapter 25:

Appreciating the Journey

"Discover the beauty in every step of the way!"

Ah, the joy of appreciating the journey! The
world is full of wonders, my friend, and it's up
to us to take notice of them and make the
most out of each and every day.

Picture this, you're on a road trip, the sun is shining, the music is blasting, and the wind is blowing through your hair. You can feel the excitement in the air as you approach your destination. But wait, why rush to the end? Why not slow down and appreciate the journey? Take a moment to really look around and touch the abundance that surrounds you. The world is full of hidden gems, just waiting for you to discover them.

For example, have you ever stopped to smell the owners on the side of the road? Their sweet fragrance can be a much-needed break from the monotony of daily life. Have you ever taken a detour to explore a small town that you've never been to before?

You might just stumble upon a quaint little Diner with the best apple pie you've ever tasted. Have you ever stopped to watch a beautiful sunset or sunrise? The colors can take your breath away and leave you in awe.

These small moments can make a big impact on our lives. They allow us to slow down and live in the present, soak up the beauty that surrounds us, and find joy in the journey. It's important to remember that life is not just about the destination, it's about the memories and experiences that we have along the way.

So, my friend, make your short trip a good one. Take the time to appreciate the journey, to look around, and touch the abundance that surrounds you. Trust me, you won't regret it. Life is a precious gift, and it's up to us to make the most out of each and every day.

Here are a few tips to help you make the most of your journey and appreciate the abundance that surrounds you:

1. Embrace the unknown: Don't be afraid to take a detour and explore new territories. Sometimes, the best experiences come from unexpected places.

2. Live in the moment: Try to be fully present in every moment. Turn off your phone and enjoy the sights, sounds, and sensations around you.

3. Be curious: Ask questions, seek out new experiences, and try new things. Curiosity can lead you to some truly amazing discoveries.

4. Practice gratitude: Take a moment each day to reflect on what you're grateful for. Appreciating the good things in life can help you feel more content and fulfilled.

5. Find joy in the simple things: Take time to enjoy the little things in life, like a beautiful sunset, a good meal, or a kind act from a stranger. These small moments can bring us great joy.

6. Connect with others: Share your experiences with friends and loved ones. Connecting with others can make the journey even more memorable and enjoyable.

Remember, the journey is just as important as the destination. By embracing these tips, you can make the most of your journey and appreciate the abundance that surrounds you. So go ahead, take a deep breath, and enjoy the ride!

Chapter 26:

The Power of Positive Thinking

"Harness the power of positive thinking -
create an epic life filled with joy, abundance,
and fulfillment"

The power of positive thinking is a formidable
force that can shape our lives in ways that are
beyond imagination. By focusing on the good
and letting go of negative thoughts, we can
create a life that is filled with happiness,
abundance, and fulfillment.

Positive thinking is not just about having a smile on your face or looking on the bright side of things, it is about a complete shift in your mindset, a new perspective that enables you to see the world in a new light.

Positive thinking is like a magnet that attracts positive experiences into our lives. When we focus on positive thoughts, we emit a vibration that attracts similar experiences into our lives. This is why it is so important to surround ourselves with positive people who support and uplift us. When we surround ourselves with positive individuals, we are surrounded by a positive energy that rubs off on us and helps us to see the world in a more positive light.

Practicing gratitude is also a key component of positive thinking. Gratitude allows us to focus on what we have, instead of what we don't have. It helps us to appreciate the small things in life, like the sunshine on our faces, a good cup of coffee, or a warm hug from a loved one. Gratitude helps us to see the silver lining in every situation and to recognize that every experience, good or bad, is an opportunity for growth and learning.

Positive thinking has the power to transform our lives in ways that we never thought possible.

It helps us to overcome challenges, to achieve our goals, and to live a life that is filled with joy and purpose. Positive thinking is not just a state of mind, it is a way of life.

So, the next time you find yourself facing a difficult situation or feeling down, remember the power of positive thinking and focus on the good. The world is full of possibilities and the power of positive thinking is all it takes to bring them to life.

If you're looking to harness the power of positive thinking and transform your life, here are some tips to get you started:

1. Focus on the good. Make a conscious effort to focus on the positive aspects of your life. Write down a list of things you are grateful for and look at it often. Celebrate your achievements, no matter how small, and acknowledge the good in every situation.

2. Let go of negative thoughts. Negative thoughts have a way of holding us back and draining our energy. When negative thoughts pop into your head, acknowledge them, but then let them go. Replace them with positive thoughts and affirmations.

3. Surround yourself with positive people. The people we surround ourselves with have a profound impact on our lives. Seek out positive individuals who lift you and support you. Surround yourself with their positive energy and let it rub off on you.

4. Practice gratitude. Gratitude is the foundation of positive thinking. Take time each day to reflect on what you are grateful for. This can be as simple as acknowledging the little things in life, like a beautiful sunset or a good cup of coffee.

5. Look for the silver lining. Every experience, good or bad, is an opportunity for growth and learning. Look for the silver lining in every situation and focus on what you can learn from it.

6. Embrace positivity. Positive thinking is a choice. Embrace positivity and make it a part of your daily routine. Repeat positive affirmations, read inspiring books, and listen to motivational speakers.

7. Celebrate the small victories. Celebrate the small victories along the way. Recognize your progress and give yourself credit for your achievements, no matter how small.

8. Practice self-care. Taking care of yourself is crucial for maintaining a positive outlook. Exercise regularly, eat a healthy diet, and make time for the things you love.

By incorporating these tips into your life, you can harness the power of positive thinking and transform your life. Positive thinking has the power to bring joy, abundance, and fulfillment into your life, so why not give it a try today?

Chapter 27:

The Importance of Self-Care

"Find Balance, Find Bliss: Embrace the Art of Self-Care."

Self-care is a critical aspect of our lives that is often neglected. As we go through our daily routines, we get caught up in the hustle and bustle of life and forget to take care of ourselves. It's easy to push aside our own needs and desires and put everyone else's needs first.

But it's essential to understand that taking care of ourselves is not selfish; it's necessary for our physical, emotional, and spiritual well-being.

Self-care involves taking the time to nurture ourselves and prioritize our own needs. It's about setting boundaries and taking control of our lives, so we don't get caught up in the never-ending cycle of stress and burnout.
When we take care of ourselves, we are better equipped to handle life's challenges, and we can show up for ourselves and others in a more authentic and meaningful way.

One of the most significant forms of self-care is physical self-care. This involves nourishing our bodies with healthy food, engaging in regular exercise, and getting enough sleep. Exercise can help reduce stress, improve mood, and boost self-esteem.

A nutritious diet provides our bodies with the essential nutrients it needs to function at its best. Getting enough sleep helps to refresh and recharge our bodies, so we have the energy to tackle each day with enthusiasm.

Emotional self-care is also crucial for our well-being. This involves taking the time to process our feelings and emotions and engage in
activities that bring us peace and calm. This could be as simple as taking a relaxing bath, journaling, or engaging in a hobby that brings us joy.

It's also important to practice self-compassion and be kind and gentle with ourselves, instead of criticizing and punishing ourselves for every little mistake.

Spiritual self-care is about connecting with something greater than ourselves and finding meaning and purpose in life. This could be through religion, spirituality, or simply spending time in nature and connecting with the natural world. Engaging in practices such as meditation and yoga can help bring a sense of peace and inner calm.

Self-care is a critical aspect of our lives that should not be overlooked. It's about taking the time to prioritize our own needs and well-being, so we can show up for ourselves and others in a more authentic and meaningful way.

So, let's make self-care a priority in our lives and engage in activities that bring us peace, joy, and fulfillment. Your well-being is worth it.

Self-care is a crucial aspect of life that should be given the attention and importance it deserves.

Here are some tips to help you take care of yourself physically, emotionally, and spiritually:

1. Set Boundaries: One of the most important things you can do for yourself is to set boundaries. This means saying no to things that don't serve you and create space for the things that do. It's essential to be honest with yourself and others about what you need and what you can handle.

2. Prioritize Self-Care: Make self-care a priority in your life. This could be as simple as taking a few minutes each day to engage in an activity that brings you peace or carving out time each week to do something you enjoy. It's important to make self-care a non-negotiable part of your routine.

3. Find Your Balance: Engage in a mix of physical, emotional, and spiritual self-care activities to achieve a balanced and well-rounded approach to self-care. This could be a combination of exercise, mindfulness practices, spending time in nature, and more.

4. Nourish Your Body: Eating a nutritious diet that is rich in vitamins and minerals is essential for physical self-care. Make sure to incorporate plenty of fruits and vegetables and limit your intake of processed foods.

5. Exercise Regularly: Regular exercise can help reduce stress, improve mood, and boost self-esteem. It doesn't have to be intense; a simple walk in the park or a yoga class can make a world of difference.

6. Get Enough Sleep: Sleep is essential for our physical and emotional well-being. Make sure to get enough sleep each night and create a relaxing bedtime routine to help you fall asleep more easily.

7. Connect with Nature: Spending time in nature has been shown to have a positive impact on our mental and emotional well-being. Take a walk in the park, go for a hike, or simply sit in your backyard and soak up the sunshine.

8. Practice Gratitude: Practicing gratitude helps us to focus on the positive aspects of our lives and helps us to cultivate a more positive outlook. Start each day by writing down three things you're grateful for or take a few minutes each evening to reflect on the good things that happened during the day.

In conclusion, self-care is a vital aspect of our lives that should be given the attention and importance it deserves. By prioritizing self-care and engaging in activities that bring us peace, joy, and fulfillment, we can show up for ourselves and others in a more authentic and meaningful way. So, let's make self-care a priority in our lives and start taking care of ourselves, both physically, emotionally, and spiritually.

Chapter 28:
Building Strong Relationships

"From strangers to lifelong friends - Connect
with the heart, listen with the soul"

Building strong relationships is an art that
requires effort, patience, and a sincere desire
to connect with others. Relationships are at
the core of our lives, providing us with love,
support, and a sense of belonging. Whether
it's our family, friends, or colleagues, the quality
of our relationships can have a profound
impact on our happiness and well-being.

The first step in building strong relationships is to be kind and compassionate towards others. People are often more likely to open up and connect with those who they feel are kind and understanding. When we take the time to listen to others and show empathy, we demonstrate that we value them as individuals and care about their feelings. By being compassionate, we can create a warm and supportive environment that encourages people to open up and share their thoughts and feelings.

Effective communication is also crucial in building strong relationships. Listening actively to what others have to say is an important part of effective communication.

It means paying attention to their words, tone, and body language to understand what they're trying to convey. When we listen actively, we're able to respond in a way that demonstrates that we understand and value their perspective.

Effective communication also involves expressing ourselves clearly and openly. We should be honest about our thoughts and feelings, and not be afraid to ask for what we

need or want from others. When we're open and honest in our communication, we build trust and mutual respect, which are essential elements of strong relationships.

Finally, strong relationships are built on trust and mutual respect. It's important to be honest and transparent with others, even if it means admitting our flaws and weaknesses. When we're honest and open about who we are, others are more likely to trust us and feel comfortable sharing their thoughts and feelings. By fostering open and honest relationships, we can build deeper connections and stronger bonds with those around us.

Building strong relationships requires effort, patience, and a sincere desire to connect with others. By being kind and compassionate, listening actively, communicating effectively, and fostering open and honest relationships, we can create the supportive and loving connections that are essential to a happy and fulfilling life.

Here are some tips if you're looking to strengthen your bonds with family, friends, or colleagues, these tips are sure to bring some spark and excitement to your interactions with others.

1. Practice Active Listening: When we listen actively to others, we show that we value their perspective and care about what they have to say. To practice active listening, put away your phone, make eye contact, and give the person your full attention.

2. Repeat what they've said in your own words to demonstrate that you understand their point of view.

3. Be Genuinely Interested: People love to talk about themselves, and when we show a genuine interest in their lives, they feel valued and appreciated. Ask questions and listen attentively to what they have to say. This creates a warm and welcoming environment where people feel comfortable opening up and sharing their thoughts and feelings.

4. Communicate Openly and Honestly: Honesty is the best policy, especially when it comes to building strong relationships. Be transparent about your thoughts, feelings, and intentions, and encourage others to do the same. When we're open and honest, we build trust and mutual respect, which are essential components of strong relationships.

5. Show Appreciation: A simple act of appreciation can go a long way in building strong relationships. Express gratitude for things others do for you, and let them know that you value their efforts. This creates a positive and supportive environment where people feel valued and appreciated.

6. Make Time for Fun: Relationships are strengthened when we have fun together. Whether it's taking a walk, having a picnic, or playing a game, make time for activities that bring joy and laughter to your interactions with others. Having fun together helps build memories and strengthens bonds.

7. Embrace Differences: Embracing differences is an important part of building strong relationships. We all have unique perspectives and ways of viewing the world. When we learn to accept and appreciate these differences, we can create a diverse and inclusive environment where everyone feels valued and appreciated.

In conclusion, building strong relationships takes effort, patience, and a sincere desire to connect with others. By practicing active listening, showing genuine interest, communicating openly and honestly, expressing appreciation, making time for fun, and embracing differences, we can create strong and meaningful relationships that bring joy and fulfillment to our lives.

Chapter 29:

Learning from Life's Challenges

"Embrace the unknown, cultivate resilience,
and unleash your full potential."

Life is a journey filled with twists and turns, ups
and downs, and unexpected challenges. These
challenges, however, are not something to be
feared or avoided. Instead, they should be
embraced as opportunities to learn and grow.

By facing life's challenges head-on, we can develop a greater understanding of ourselves and the world around us, as well as build important skills such as resilience, determination, and problem-solving.

One of the keys to learning from life's challenges is to maintain a positive outlook and persevere through difficult times. This requires a strong sense of self-belief and an unwavering commitment to our goals, even when things get tough. It is important to remind ourselves that we have the strength and ability to overcome any obstacle and that the lessons we learn from these experiences will only make us stronger in the long run.

Another important aspect of learning from life's challenges is to celebrate our successes, no matter how small they may seem. This helps to build our confidence and motivation, as well as gives us a sense of pride in our progress. Whether it's accomplishing a difficult task, making a new friend, or simply making it through a trying day, it is important to acknowledge and celebrate our successes along the way.

Ultimately, the key to learning from life's challenges is to approach each one with an open mind and a willingness to learn and grow.

By embracing challenges as opportunities for growth and celebrating our successes, we can not only overcome the difficulties we face but also gain a deeper understanding of ourselves and the world around us.

So let us embrace each new challenge with excitement and eagerness, confident in the knowledge that we have the skills and determination to overcome whatever comes our way.

Here are some tips that have worked for me and may help you as well:

1. Embrace a growth mindset: Instead of viewing challenges as insurmountable obstacles, adopt a growth mindset and see them as opportunities to learn and grow.

2. By doing so, you'll be more likely to tackle these challenges with determination and a positive attitude.

3. Practice resilience: Life is full of ups and downs, and it's important to be able to bounce back from setbacks. Cultivate resilience by developing a positive outlook, seeking support from others when you need it, and learning from your experiences.

4. Celebrate your successes: No matter how small they may seem, it's important to acknowledge and celebrate your successes along the way. This helps to build confidence, motivation, and a sense of pride in your progress.

5. Seek out new experiences: Embrace new experiences and challenges, as they provide opportunities for growth and learning. Whether it's trying a new hobby or taking on a difficult task, stepping outside of your comfort zone can help you grow in unexpected ways.

6. Reflect on your experiences: Take the time to reflect on your experiences, both the good and the bad. By doing so, you'll be able to gain insights into what worked and what didn't and use this information to continue growing and improving.

7. Stay positive: Maintaining a positive attitude, even in the face of difficult challenges, is key to learning and growing. Surround yourself with positive, supportive people and engage in activities that bring you joy and help you maintain a positive outlook.

By following these tips, you can turn life's challenges into opportunities for growth and learning. Remember, life is a journey, not a destination, and each challenge is simply a step along the way. So, embrace each new challenge with excitement and eagerness, and never stop growing and learning!

Chapter 30:
Living with Purpose and Passion

"Believe in yourself, the sky's the limit."

Living with purpose and passion is not just a
motto or a catchphrase, it's a way of life that
can bring true happiness and fulfillment. It's
about finding what ignites your soul, what
makes you feel alive, and making that the
driving force behind your daily existence.
When you live with purpose and passion, you
are in tune with your values, your beliefs, and
your desires. You have a clear direction, a

reason for being, and a sense of fulfillment that comes from knowing you are living a life that is true to who you are.

The journey of discovering your purpose and passion can be a thrilling and life-changing experience. It requires a level of introspection, self-selection, and a willingness to step out of your comfort zone and try new things. It's about getting in touch with your innermost desires, your strengths, and what brings you joy and satisfaction. Once you've opportunities to learn and grow. Keep in mind that living with purpose and passion is not found what lights you up, it's about taking action, setting goals, and continuously pushing yourself to grow and evolve.

Believe in yourself and your abilities. Trust that the journey ahead is full of opportunities for growth and learning. Don't be afraid to fail, embrace challenges and setbacks as

a destination, but a journey that is constantly evolving and changing. Stay open to new experiences and be willing to pivot and adjust your course as needed.

fulfillment to your life. It's about finding what sets your soul on fire, aligning your life with

your values, and continuously setting new goals and pushing yourself to grow. Believe in yourself and your abilities and trust the journey ahead.

Embrace challenges and setbacks as opportunities to learn and grow and stay open to new experiences. So, go ahead and make the most of your life by living with purpose and passion.

Living with purpose and passion is a noble pursuit, but it's not always an easy journey. Here are some tips and takeaways from this chapter to help you on your way:

One of the key elements of living with purpose and passion is aligning your life with your values. This means taking the time to define what's important to you and making sure that your actions and decisions align with those values.

It's about prioritizing what's meaningful to you and being intentional about the way you live your life. Whether it's your relationships, your career, your hobbies, or your community, make sure that you are investing your time and energy in the things that matter most to you.

Living with purpose and passion is a journey that can bring true happiness and

1. Get in touch with your innermost desires: Take the time to reflect on what makes you happy, what brings you joy, and what you're truly passionate about. Write down your thoughts, meditate, and do whatever it takes to get in touch with your innermost desires.

2. Align your life with your values: Once you know what you're passionate about, it's time to align your life with your values. Make sure that your actions and decisions reflect what's important to you and prioritize the things that matter most.

3. Set goals and push yourself to grow: Having a clear direction and purpose is great, but it's not enough. Continuously set new goals and challenge yourself to grow. This will keep you motivated and help you achieve your dreams.

4. Believe in yourself and your abilities: Trust that you have what it takes to succeed, and don't be afraid to step out of your comfort zone. Believe in yourself and your abilities and trust the journey ahead.

5. Embrace challenges and setbacks: Don't be afraid of failure. Embrace challenges and setbacks as opportunities to learn and grow. These experiences can help you develop resilience and strength and will make you a better, more well-rounded person.

6. Stay open to new experiences: Living with purpose and passion requires a willingness to be open to new experiences. Stay curious, try new things, and be willing to pivot and adjust your course as needed.

7. Surround yourself with positive people: Surround yourself with people who support and encourage you. Seek out mentors and role models who can provide guidance and inspiration.

8. Celebrate your successes: Make sure to celebrate your successes along the way. Whether it's big or small, take the time to acknowledge and appreciate your accomplishments.

Living with purpose and passion is a journey worth pursuing. By getting in touch with your innermost desires, aligning your life with your values, setting goals and pushing yourself to grow, believing in yourself and your abilities, embracing challenges and setbacks, staying open to new experiences, surrounding yourself with positive people, and celebrating your successes, you can create a life that is fulfilling, meaningful, and true to who you are. So, go ahead and start your journey today!

In Conclusion,

The Blueprint for Success: "The Secret Roadmap for Living Your Best Life, Gaining Wealth" is your comprehensive guide to unlocking your inner wealth and unleashing an abundant life. Through its 30 chapters, you have explored various themes and principles that can help you achieve success, happiness, and fulfillment in all areas of your life.

From defining wealth to mastering the law of vibration, this book provides a roadmap for creating a life filled with abundance, joy, and positive energy.

Throughout the book it emphasizes the importance of having a growth mindset, gratitude, clarity, and self-love. You are encouraged to embrace self-care, your life's purpose, and pursue your dreams passionately. It highlights the power of positive thinking, forgiveness, and the importance of balancing both masculine and feminine energy.

In the end, The Blueprint for Success is a reminder that the journey to abundance and joy starts with a clear vision, self-awareness, and a willingness to embrace change. Whether you are seeking to elevate your financial future, deepen your relationships, or live a life filled with purpose and passion, always come back to this book as it provides a roadmap to help you get there.

So, embrace the journey, celebrate your wins, and live life to the fullest!

Acknowledgments

This book would not have been possible without the unwavering support and encouragement of so many incredible individuals. I extend my deepest gratitude to my family, friends, and mentors, whose belief in me has been a constant source of inspiration. Your guidance and love have fueled my determination and passion every step of the way.

To the readers who have chosen to embark on this journey, thank you for trusting me to be a part of your path to success. Your dreams are the driving force behind my mission, and it is my deepest hope that this book empowers you to unlock your true potential.

A special thanks to the talented individuals who supported the creation of this book. Your dedication and commitment to helping others achieve personal growth and financial empowerment are truly inspiring. Together, we are creating a future where everyone has the tools to thrive.

About the Author

Chad T is a visionary entrepreneur, author, and motivational leader. With a passion for financial empowerment and personal development, Chad combines his expertise in innovative strategies and motivational tools to help individuals achieve their goals.

Through his writing, Chad aims to inspire, motivate, and guide readers on their journey to success, blending practical insights with actionable strategies for personal and financial growth. His vision extends beyond individual achievements; it's about fostering a global movement of empowerment, innovation, and community-driven success.

A Final Note

Thank you for reading this book. Your journey doesn't end here—it's just the beginning. If you found this book valuable, please consider leaving a review. Your feedback helps others discover the tools they need to unlock their potential and transform their lives.

Explore more titles from the *Wealth Accelerator Book Series* and continue your journey toward personal and financial growth. Together, let's turn our dreams into reality.

Copyright Notice

Disclaimer

53469828R00089